DETROIT PUBLIC LIBRARY

3 5674 03567848 2

W9-BXM-795

KNAPP BRANCH LIBRARY
13330 CONANT
DETROIT, MI 48212
852-4283

AUG 02

KN

MEGATECH

BioTech

Frontiers of medicine

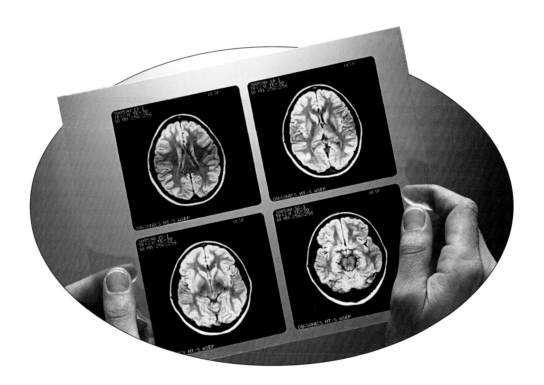

David Jefferis

Crabtree
www.crabtreebooks.com

Introduction

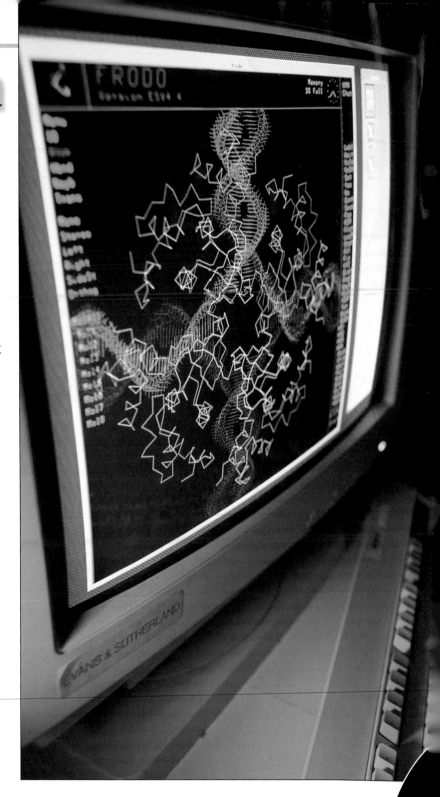

B iotech is short for biotechnology, the area of science that links biology and technology. Biotech is a new field, where researchers find ways that natural living things can be altered or improved by science and engineering.

Our bodies are made of billions of tiny **cells**. In these cells are **genes**, which control how our bodies develop. Using genes to create new types of living things is called **genetic engineering**. It is one of the most important areas of biotech.

There are other branches of biotech – for example, the field of biomechanics provides athletes with better clothes and equipment. Bionics and **prosthetics** replace damaged or failing body parts with high-tech machines.

Crabtree Publishing Company
PMB 16A,   612 Welland Avenue
350 Fifth Avenue   St Catharines
Suite 3308   Ontario
New York   L2M 5V6
NY 10118

Edited by
Isabella McIntyre
Coordinating Editor
Ellen Rodger
Project Editor
Kate Calder

Assistant Editors
P. A. Finlay
Carrie Gleason
Production Coordinator
Rosie Gowsell

Technical consultant
Gerard Cheshire BSc

Picture research by
Kay Rowley

Created and produced by
Alpha Communications in association
with Firecrest Books Ltd.

©2002 David Jefferis/Alpha
Communications

Cataloging-in-Publication Data
Jefferis, David.
    Bio Tech: frontiers of medicine/
David Jefferis.
    p. cm -- (Megatech)
    Includes index.
    Summary:Presents the field of
biotechnology, which links biology and
technology, discussing how living things
can be altered by science and
engineering.
    ISBN 0-7787-0051-8 (rlb) -- ISBN
0-7787-0061-5 (pbk.)
    1. Biotechnology--Juvenile
literature. [1. Biotechnology.] I. Title. II.
Series.
    TP248.218.J44 2002
    660.6--dc21
                2001037086
                LC

Prepress
Embassy Graphics

Printed by
Worzalla Publishing Company

All rights reserved. No part of this
publication may be reproduced, stored
in any retrieval system or transmitted
in any form, by any means, electronic,
photographic, recording or otherwise,
except brief extracts for the purposes of
review, without the written permission
of the publisher and copyright holder.

Pictures on these pages, clockwise
from far left:
1   Robot arm tests DNA samples.
2   Researcher uses 3D goggles to
view a biotech computer image.
3   Capsule containing
medicine in hundreds of
tiny balls.
4   Computer image showing
blood flowing through the
heart
5   Computer scan showing
the inside of a human body.

Previous page shows:
Computer scan of a
patient's brain.

Contents

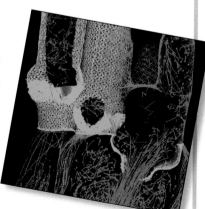

Medical advance

Biotechnology is at the cutting edge of medicine, but it is a recent branch of science. In the old days, patients' lives were often ended by the doctors who were trying to save them.

▲ *In the Middle Ages, medical research was carried out by pharmacists, called apothecaries. Finding a medicine that worked well was done through a process of trial and error.*

A century ago, disease and injury were serious matters. There was little knowledge of how disease was spread and no **anesthetic** to keep patients unconscious during operations. British surgeon Sir Joseph Lister was the first to use **antiseptics** to kill **bacteria** while he was operating on patients, in the mid-1800s. Until then, surviving an operation was a matter of luck in avoiding disease and being strong enough to withstand the pain.

▲ *Helping injured soldiers in battle was difficult, and there were few ways to relieve pain. Above, a surgeon prepares for an outdoor operation in 1863, during the U.S. Civil War.*

Early surgical instruments made of steel and wood

◄ *These were some of the best instruments available in 1782. This book was a surgeon's guide from that time.*

▲ *In 1790, French army surgeons introduced the world's first ambulance. The covered cart carried surgical instruments and two wounded soldiers.*

▲ *Modern technology makes operations safer. Above, a surgeon operates in a special operating room, sealed to keep out bacteria. In the future, advances in biotechnology will mean doctors do fewer traditional operations.*

Today, understanding how living things work has become one of the most important areas of scientific research. Many doctors believe that health care will go through more changes in the next 30 years than it has in the last 2000 years. One welcome change will be in surgery. It will become far less common because new medicines will control diseases and their symptoms.

What is an X-ray?

X-rays *are a type of radiation that can be used to take pictures of people's bones. X-rays were discovered in 1895 by a German scientist, Wilhelm Roentgen.*

X-rays pass easily through soft body tissues, such as skin, but are stopped by solid material, such as bone. This means that X-rays can be used to check bones and teeth without surgery. Unfortunately, too many X-rays can be dangerous to health, so doctors limit the number a person can have.

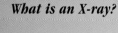

Soft tissue appears as a ghostly image in this X-ray. Bones are more visible

Secrets of the cell

Cells are the building blocks of life. All living things, from tiny fleas to giant redwood trees, are made of cells. The center of each cell contains material that controls life itself.

▲ *This is a stem cell. In our bodies, these develop into different types of cells, which form eyes, ears, bones, and other parts of the body.*

Until the 1600s, no one knew that there were things so small you could not see them with the human eye. In 1608, Zacharias Jansen from Holland invented the microscope, and began a voyage of discovery into the micro-universe. In 1665, Robert Hooke, an English physicist, published a book called *Micrographia*. It was packed with drawings Hooke had made of things he saw through the microscope. He noticed that a slice of cork was made up of many little box shapes, which he called cells. Later, researchers found that there were many different cells, and that some simple organisms were made of just one cell.

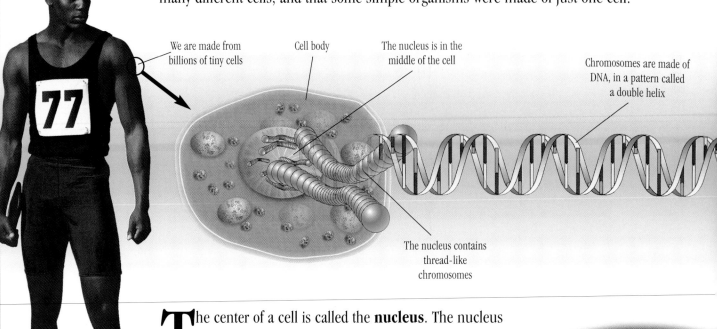

We are made from billions of tiny cells

Cell body

The nucleus is in the middle of the cell

Chromosomes are made of DNA, in a pattern called a double helix

The nucleus contains thread-like chromosomes

The center of a cell is called the **nucleus**. The nucleus contains tiny thread-like particles called **chromosomes**. Chromosomes are made mostly of a spiral-shaped **molecule** called DeoxyriboNucleic Acid, or **DNA**. DNA carries patterns of chemicals called sequences. The patterns are known as gene sequences and they carry the instructions for life – from the color of an apple to the stripes of a zebra.

▶ *This tiny single-cell creature called a radiolarian lives in the sea.*

What is a genome?

A genome is the complete set of gene instructions for a particular species, whether it is a gorilla or a grasshopper.

Several genomes are already known – those of fruit flies and worms were completed in 1998. The genomes of other species have also been studied.

Considering the difference in how life forms look, it is surprising how similar the genomes often are. For example, the genomes of humans and chimpanzees are very similar. All but 1.5 percent of the DNA is the same.

A gorilla and a grasshopper each have a different genome

DNA spirals are joined by rungs called base pairs, or genes

DNA can divide to copy itself

Gene patterns are coded messages that define living things

◀ *Organisms grow when their cells divide. One cell becomes two cells. The DNA also divides to make a copy of itself, so the genetic instructions are carried by the new cell as well as the old one.*

Discovering what the gene sequences do, and how to use them, is the work of biotechnologists. Different gene sequences carry different messages, and the DNA carries those messages. A biotech researcher may take a gene instruction from the DNA of one **species** and put it into another, to make a different organism. For example, genetically modified plants, or **GM** plants, may include genes that give the plants resistance to disease, or a longer shelf life. Some tomatoes have been made with genes that enable them to be stored without ripening too soon.

▶ *Tomatoes were one of the earliest plants to be genetically modified.*

Making medicines

The medicine in this capsule is released from tiny balls as the capsule dissolves slowly in the stomach.

People have been taking various traditional and herbal medicines for thousands of years. Recently, researchers found out exactly how they affect the body. Today, making medicines is an enormous industry.

The earliest known medicine users were the ancient Greeks 2500 years ago. At that time, the physician Hippocrates found that bark from the willow tree could be chewed or made into a potion that cured headaches and fevers.

Discovering exactly what ingredient in willow bark eased pain took a long time. In 1899, the German company Bayer discovered what it was, processed it, and sold it as a powdered medicine. Bayer called it aspirin.

The equipment used for preparing drugs is often delicate and expensive.

A box of aspirin powder, first sold in 1899. Aspirin was later made into pills for easier swallowing.

The useful ingredient in aspirin is called salicylic acid

The medicine-making, or pharmaceutical, industry is huge. The world's pharmaceutical companies sell medicines worth over $400 billion a year. Most of these medicines are bought by people in the world's wealthiest countries. Millions of people cannot afford to pay for life-saving, or pain-relieving medicines. One reason for the high price of drugs is that new medicines are expensive to research and develop. Drug companies spend millions of dollars to create one drug.

When can a new medicine be sold?

Each year, hundreds of medicines, ranging from painkillers to heart and cancer drugs, are produced by pharmaceutical companies.

It takes years for a new medicine to become available to the public. Along the way, drugs are tested. Drug tests, or trials, are carried out with volunteers, who take the drug to see if it is safe and effective. If the trials are successful and there is government approval, the new medicine can be sold to the public. The entire process, from research and laboratory work to the selling of a new drug, usually takes about 12 years.

Modern equipment has sped up many areas of testing, but trials with volunteer patients still take many years

Computer technology is a big help when developing new treatments. Computers can save time by predicting how a new drug might work in a patient's body. Robotic systems can carry out tests very quickly. One company estimates that testing with robots is 10,000 times quicker than doing the same testing by hand. New equipment can also tailor drugs exactly to a patient's needs, reducing waste and unwanted side effects.

▶ *Only a few of the many drugs developed will ever go on sale. Drugs must go through trials before they can be marketed and sold. Today, the world's best-selling medicine is Zantac, which helps relieve stomach ulcers.*

Spare parts

The practice of making replacement limbs and other body parts is centuries old. But the wooden legs, arms with hooks, and wooden teeth of the past did not look or act like the real thing. Today, artificial limbs are more real looking and easier to use.

▲ *Computers can show how blood moves through the heart. The information is useful when developing artificial heart valves for people who have suffered heart attacks.*

In the past, artificial limbs were heavy, ugly, and difficult to use. Today, prosthetics, the science of making replacement limbs, uses computer technology to develop more lifelike limbs.

Computers can copy the way the brain controls movement. For example, fitting a hand with pressure **sensors** on the fingers enables the hand to hold an egg gently. Adding a heat sensor causes the hand to let go if the egg is too hot to hold. Other sensors are being developed to give people an artificial sense of touch.

▲ *Dr. Peter Kyberd shows the artificial hand he has developed. A micro-computer flexes the hand and controls its finger and thumb. If the hand slips, the computer adjusts the grip pressure.*

◄ *Artificial limbs are not new. The Romans often made them for soldiers injured in battle. The limbs in this old illustration were made by the French surgeon Ambrose Paré in the 1500s.*

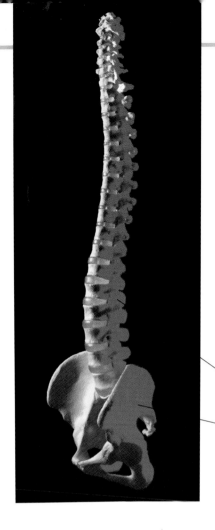

◀ *Damage to nerves in the spine can cause a person to become paralyzed. Scientists are doing research on full-body transplants to find a cure for paralysis.*

Spine

Pelvis

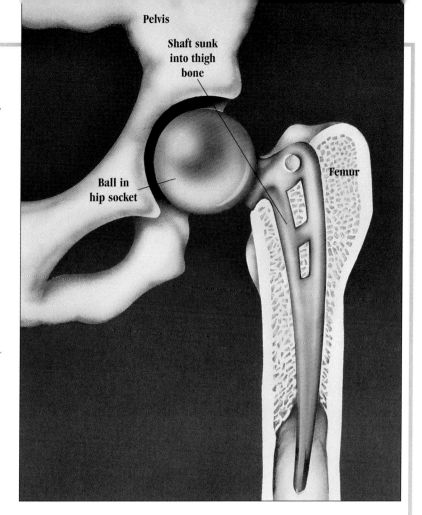

Pelvis

Shaft sunk into thigh bone

Ball in hip socket

Femur

One of the most advanced prosthetics is the FreeHand, developed by a team of U.S. researchers. It is designed to work like the human brain and sends electrical signals to muscles, making them move. In a paralyzed person, the nerve pathways from the brain to parts of the body do not work. FreeHand's computer translates a small shoulder movement into a set of tiny electric shocks, which are sent to muscles in the hand. The fingers react by grasping and pinching. To users, it is a scientific miracle, which lets them do things such as use the phone or brush their teeth.

▲ *Hip replacements are common for older people with stiff or painful joints. The hip bones move around a metal ball which is on a shaft sunk deep into the thigh bone. Sometimes the cement holding the shaft comes loose. An operation is then needed to fix it.*

Is it possible to grow spare body parts?

Researchers can now repair broken bones in animals by encouraging the growth of new bone material. They have experimented on dogs with broken legs by building an artificial section which bridges the break in the bone. The existing pieces of bone are pinned firmly in position, so they cannot move. The artificial section is called a scaffold, and it is covered in material that encourages bone to grow. New bone grows into the scaffold, and eventually replaces it. The scaffold then dissolves. The result is a brand-new bone! It is not a quick process. A bad break could take several months to regrow.

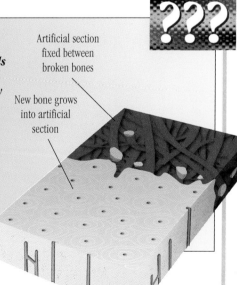

Artificial section fixed between broken bones

New bone grows into artificial section

Robo hospital

Computers and robots already help in many surgical operations. In the future, robots are likely to be even more useful, making high risk operations much easier and safer.

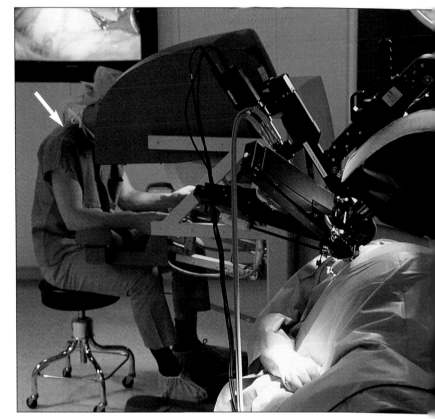

▲ *A future nano-sub could be injected into an artery to deliver a drug "torpedo" to an exact point inside the body.*

One of the most advanced robot systems is the da Vinci robot (right). The da Vinci allows a surgeon to operate through a tiny hole. This is known as **keyhole surgery**. Instead of making a large incision, the surgeon can operate through a hole as small as half an inch (12 mm) wide.

Surgical tools and a tiny video camera are attached to the ends of da Vinci's arms. The surgeon, shown by the arrow, guides the arms using TV screens that show live images from inside the patient's body. The surgeon controls the robot's arms from his desk.

Keyhole surgery has many advantages. It is far more precise than using human hands and a scalpel. There is less pain, and the risk of infection is reduced. After the operation, the patient heals faster and can go home sooner.

Robotic surgical systems cost a lot for a hospital to purchase, but the benefits of fewer infections and faster healing far outweigh the expense.

▲ *Prevention is better than cure, so many doctors recommend eating a lot of fresh fruit and vegetables.*

◄ *"Smart" toothbrushes will have a micro-computer that checks the health of teeth and gums.*

Probe measurements are fed into a computer for storage

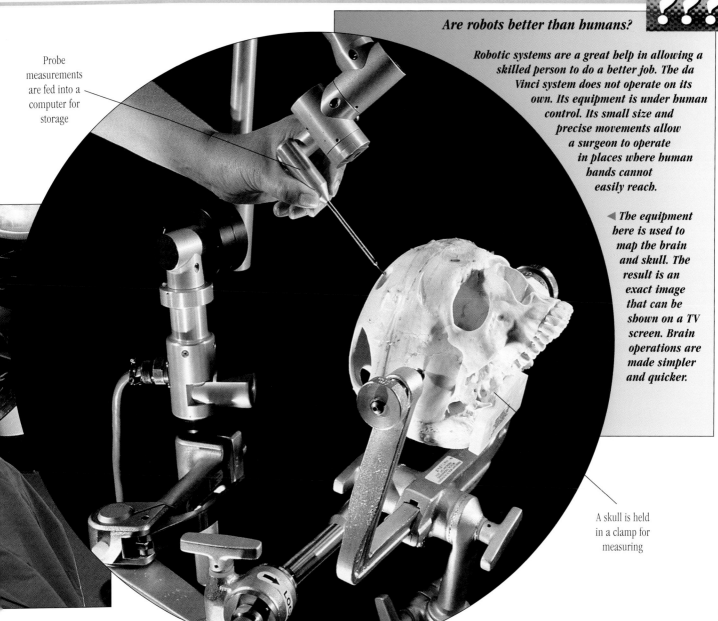

Are robots better than humans?

Robotic systems are a great help in allowing a skilled person to do a better job. The da Vinci system does not operate on its own. Its equipment is under human control. Its small size and precise movements allow a surgeon to operate in places where human hands cannot easily reach.

◀ *The equipment here is used to map the brain and skull. The result is an exact image that can be shown on a TV screen. Brain operations are made simpler and quicker.*

A skull is held in a clamp for measuring

R esearchers are now working on a number of very small machines called **nano**machines. One of these is a tiny submarine smaller than a fly speck. The nano-sub is designed to be injected into a patient's blood stream. The device then travels inside the body to deliver medicine where it is needed. The purpose of the nano-sub is to reduce the need for surgery.

▶ *Detailed computer images of a patient's body parts help identify problems.*

Super senses

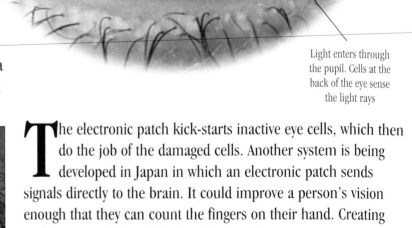

Bioengineers are developing ways of helping people with a sense that is either lost or damaged. Enhanced senses, such as super hearing or sight, are also possibilities in the future.

▲ An enlarged view of a computer chip. These lie at the heart of all biotech implants.

Our eyes register images when light goes through the pupil to fall on the **retina** at the back of the eyeball. Light-sensitive cells then send these messages to the brain.

▲ Light-sensitive cells at the back of the eye are called rods and cones because of their shape.

Bioengineers are experimenting with ways to cure blindness or improve sight. One solution is a system that works like a video camera, with an electronic patch in the back of the eye.

Light enters through the pupil. Cells at the back of the eye sense the light rays

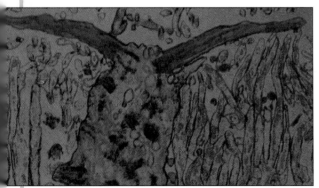

The electronic patch kick-starts inactive eye cells, which then do the job of the damaged cells. Another system is being developed in Japan in which an electronic patch sends signals directly to the brain. It could improve a person's vision enough that they can count the fingers on their hand. Creating perfect vision for the blind could take 30 years.

◄ A closeup of an olfactory receptor, or smell-cell, in your nose. An electronic version used by food companies helps check food quality.

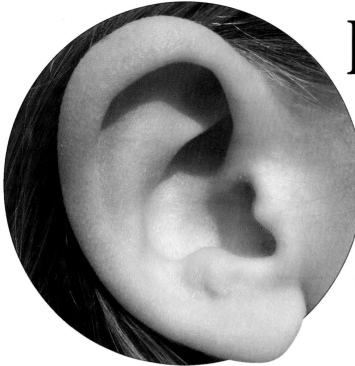

Hearing is another challenge for biotech researchers. Hearing aids have been made for many years and work by amplifying sound, or turning up the volume. One common cause of deafness is damaged or dead **hair cells** deep in the ear. Hair cells enable us to hear by picking up noise vibrations that are translated into electrical signals and then sent to the brain. Unlike many other cells, ear hair cells do not regrow.

Bioengineers are looking for a gene that can be inserted into the ear to encourage hair cells to grow again. This would restore hearing, without the need for mechanical help.

▲ *You are born with about 16,000 noise-detecting hair cells in your ears. They are easily damaged by such things as loud noise.*

Small lumps on the tongue are called **papillae**

Biotech research gives hope for people who have lost one or more of their senses. In the future, curing deafness may be no more complicated than putting gene-drops in the affected ear.

Scientists are also working on building super senses. By the middle of this century, it may be possible to see in the dark like a cat, hear distant noises better than an owl, or sniff faint aromas as well as a dog can.

◄ ▲ *You taste things with cells like this. Hundreds of these cells are on the surface of some papillae, the lumps on your tongue.*

Can animals regrow hair cells?

Some animals can regrow hair cells for hearing. Sharks, for example, grow hair cells all their lives, for a total of 100,000 cells or more, depending on the type of shark. Other animals regrow them too, including chickens and some fish. Researchers looking into causes of human deafness have studied these animals. Finding one correct gene may encourage hair cells to grow again.

Other researchers think an electronic solution may be easier and just as good – a tiny microphone patch could be attached to the surface of the inner ear, and this would send signals directly to the brain.

Most sharks have very good hearing, useful for hunting prey

Biotech boom

Many companies around the world sell products that have been developed using biotechnology.

▲ *The first* mammal *to be cloned was a sheep.*

Biotech companies have a list of products that is growing fast. For example, a French team has discovered a treatment for obesity, or being very overweight. The team has developed a drug called Famoxin, which speeds up metabolism, the body's way of burning fat. Researchers hope an overweight person might need just one injection each month to stay slim.

In the drug trials, the drug proved to be more effective when combined with exercise and a low-fat diet.

◄ *Spider silk is a tough fiber that researchers are genetically modifying to make consumer products.*

Mixing a spider gene with those of a goat sounds unlikely, yet that is what a Canadian company has done. The idea is that goat's milk will include super strong spider silk **protein**, which can be woven to form BioSteel, a fiber stronger and lighter than steel. The material will be useful for things that need strength and lightness, such as aircraft, rockets, or race cars. There are medical uses for the silk as well. Researchers hope to use it for artificial tendons, ligaments, and limbs.

▼ *Biotech experiments are mostly done in clean-room conditions. Clean rooms are rooms that are sealed to prevent bacteria growth from contaminating samples. Below, a pharmaceutical worker wears a bio-suit. Air comes through the sealed tube at the back.*

A group of growing cells is called an embryo

What is cloning?

A clone is a copy of a living thing that has the same genes as one parent. In sexual reproduction, genes from both male and female parents are mixed to create children who have genes from both their father and mother. A biotech clone has the genes of only one parent, so it is genetically identical to that parent. A natural clone is an identical twin where the egg has split after fertilization, separating into two embryos that have the same genes.

Biotechnologists want to create clones because they have specific desirable characteristics. For instance, they might clone a cow that is a good milk producer. Biotechnologists select the genes that go into a clone's DNA so that they can control exactly what will be produced.

M uch of this work is possible because of the Human Genome Organization, an international group of scientists working to sequence our genes. Scientists expect there will be many uses for genetic information.

▼ *Robot equipment can work faster than humans, speeding up many research projects.*

The helmet is sealed so the worker's breath does not escape into the research area

◄ *Movie makers have used biotech as the basis for science fiction stories. Both the human heroine and the alien monster of the movie "Alien Resurrection" are clones.*

PLATE 14

Living longer

Some animals live much longer than humans. Researchers are trying to unlock their secrets of long life so that humans can live longer, healthier lives.

▲ *Experiments show that fruit flies live longer when kept in a cool refrigerator.*

▲ *The Galapagos giant tortoise can live for nearly 300 years.*

The life span of humans is normally less than 100 years. Animals that live longer than humans include deep-sea tubeworms that can live up to 250 years, and the Galapagos giant tortoises that can live up to 300 years. Bristlecone pine trees, which grow high in the mountains of Nevada and California, are some of the oldest living things on Earth. Some of these trees are almost 5000 years old.

◄ *Research suggests that older parents live longer than teenage parents. There may be genetic reasons for this or it may be because older people are likely to have more money. More money can mean less stress when bringing up a baby. Stress can shorten lives.*

Telomeres (shown in pink) protect the ends of chromosomes.

Is there a biological clock?

Researchers have not yet found anything that predicts the length of a life. The nearest thing to a biological clock could be on the ends of chromosomes, pictured at left. The end caps of chromosomes are called telomeres, and they shorten every time a cell divides – which it does as it grows. Eventually the telomeres get too short and the cell becomes inactive or dies.

No one has yet proved that short telomeres actually are a biological clock, but in tests some normal cells have lived longer when their telomeres were reactivated.

Cloned mice are checked to see if they grow old normally. So far, the clones' lifespans are the same as those of ordinary mice.

▼ *Humans go through several stages before growth stops in the late teen years. In middle age and old age hair thins, hearing is less sensitive, bones are more brittle, and muscles become weaker.*

Five months

Eight months

Two years

Five years

Nine years

◄ *Some animals have brief lives. Many butterflies live for only a few weeks.*

The oldest human on record is Jeanne Calment, who was 122 years old at her death in 1998. She said her long life was due to "olive oil, wine, and a sense of humor." Researchers believe that a healthy diet and active lifestyle help people live longer. Jeanne learned sword fighting at the age of 85, so she certainly kept active!

Researchers study the genes of elderly people for clues to long life. If they discover genes that contribute to long life, they will try to use their research to prolong the lives of other people.

▶ *We need oxygen to live, but oxygen also damages cells. Birds burn oxygen faster than humans and have less-damaged cells. This helps scientists understand aging.*

Biotech kitchen

Biotech engineers have created plants with built-in resistance to insect attacks and diseases. In the future, people might buy foods that include medicine as an ingredient.

▲ *GM foods can be made in different colors, but poor sales of bread dyed in bright colors in the 1950s proved that people do not want food that looks too different.*

Biotech food is not new. In 1992, tobacco farmers in China planted crops with altered genes that had greater disease resistance. Two years later, "Flavr Savr" tomatoes were planted in the U.S. The tomatoes were modified so they did not soften and rot as quickly as normal tomatoes. Since then, many other genetically modified, or GM, crops have been planted. Today, the leading GM crops are corn, soybeans, and cotton.

GM foods have raised controversy. Some people say GM crops are better for the environment, because plants with built-in resistance to disease do not need as many pesticides. Other people worry that strange genes may damage the environment. Some feel that not enough research has been done on the long-term effects these foods have on humans.

▲ *Researchers have inserted genes in some varieties of potato that act as medicine. This enables you to eat medicine rather than take it in pills or by injections.*

◄ *Over half of the foods on sale in North American supermarkets have GM ingredients.*

Nutraceuticals combine food value with medicine. One company has produced a GM pizza which is low in fat, to keep weight down, and high in calcium, which is good for teeth and bones. The pizza also has extra protein, which is good for muscles, and lycopene from GM tomatoes. Lycopene is the pigment that makes tomatoes red and is also thought to be good for the heart. Will such nutraceuticals catch on? Time will tell!

◄ *Many people believe that foods are best made in traditional ways, without any GM ingredients.*

Will we eat meat in the future?

Early humans hunted for their food, and meat was a vital part of their diet. Meat is still important to most of us, but for people who do not like GM products, much of the meat on sale in supermarkets today is not appealing.

A typical food animal may have been fed with GM grain, pumped with medicine to keep it healthy, and given injections to make it grow quickly. Many people think that meat would be better for us if the animals were raised organically – free to walk around in fields, and with no GM food, chemicals, or other artificial ingredients to make them grow.

This cow was raised on pesticide-free **organic food**

Keeping food fresh has been a concern ever since the days of sailing ships, when meat was preserved in salt to stop it from rotting on long ocean voyages. The invention of the refrigerator in 1851 was a landmark in food preservation.

Even with refrigeration, lettuce kept in a bag still turns brown and rots after about two weeks. The problem is that the lettuce is alive when it is cut at the root and bagged for sale. When the lettuce has used up the air in the bag, it quickly rots and dies. Biotech researchers have come up with a clever idea – the breathing bag. This bag is made of material that takes in air at the same rate as the cut vegetable, which doubles the vegetable's storage life.

◀ ▼ *Breathable bags reduce waste in the supermarket, and allow plenty of storage time in the refrigerator before the vegetables need to be eaten.*

Fresh lettuce when bought

Lettuce after two weeks in a non-breathing bag

◀ *GM pizza is just one nutraceutical food. Other ideas being tested include foods with additives that improve athletic performance.*

▼ *The most common GM crop is corn. Farmers planted a lot of GM corn in the 1990s, but people in many countries did not like the idea of eating it.*

Can we cure?

▲ *There is no cure for the common cold, although scientists have tried to find one for many years.*

Even with the power of biotechnology, it is not possible to say we will cure every disease. But many diseases may be treated more effectively in the near future.

Cancer is a group of cells that grow out of control. Some do little harm but others become killers. Doctors try to find cancer in a patient early and usually use drugs to fight it. Among the possible future cures for cancer is the bio-engineered P53 gene. This gene is designed to find cancer cells like a torpedo finds a target. Other treatments include injections that starve cancerous cells.

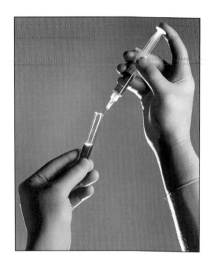

▶ *In the future, cancers may be treated using injections that cut off their blood supply.*

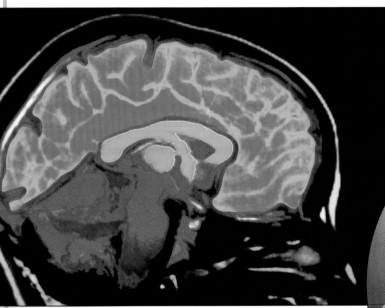

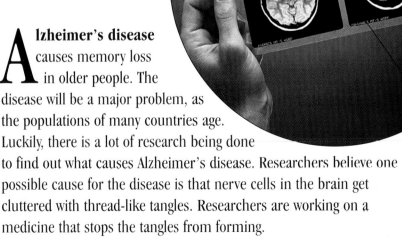

▲ *If no cure is found for Alzheimer's disease, by 2025 there could be eight million sufferers in the United States alone, with millions more around the world.*

Alzheimer's disease causes memory loss in older people. The disease will be a major problem, as the populations of many countries age. Luckily, there is a lot of research being done to find out what causes Alzheimer's disease. Researchers believe one possible cause for the disease is that nerve cells in the brain get cluttered with thread-like tangles. Researchers are working on a medicine that stops the tangles from forming.

Brain scans are used to check on Alzheimer's disease

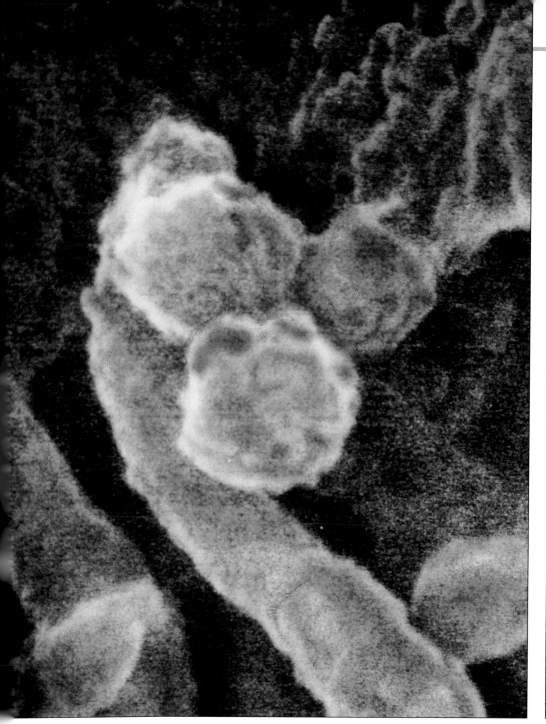

The pink blobs in this magnified photograph are HIV viruses. They are in the early stages of attacking a red blood cell.

Are alternative medicines useful?

Herbal remedies, such as ginseng and ginkgo, are old fashioned compared to the latest biotech medicines. Yet millions of people use alternative medicines every day. Researchers are working to find out how they work. Herbal remedies that perform well will be added to the range of standard medical treatments.

The sunflower plant supplies various extracts, including echinacea, for colds.

T he **AIDS** virus is one of the world's greatest problems. The virus erodes the body's **immune system**, leaving people with AIDS defenseless against invading micro-organisms that cause sickness. By the beginning of the twenty-first century, 15 million people had died from AIDS. Many more will die if a cure is not found.

A virus called HIV is the cause of AIDS, and over a dozen drugs have been developed to treat AIDS patients. These drugs are not a complete cure, and millions of people with HIV and AIDS in Africa and Asia cannot afford the expensive drug treatments developed and used in North America and Europe.

▲ *Jet flights allow infections to travel quickly around the world as travelers carry viruses to different countries.*

23

Super sports

▲ *Swimmers used to shave their bodies, so they would move through the water smoothly and quickly. Now they wear full-body suits that give them even more speed.*

Science is now used to improve performance in all sorts of sporting events.

In the sporting world, taking drugs to improve performance is banned, whether it is to lift heavier weights, run faster, or to help a horse win a race. The rule makers say that using drugs is cheating.

Researchers help in other ways, such as by developing new materials for clothing and equipment. Studying the way athletes move their bodies leads to more efficient movements, for better performance in competition.

▶ *Running is a simple sport. It does not need much equipment except for a good pair of shoes. Running shoes are constantly being improved.*

Firm arch support stops feet from rolling inward

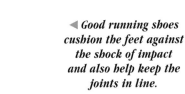

◀ *Good running shoes cushion the feet against the shock of impact and also help keep the joints in line.*

▶ *Running shoes have a number of parts, designed for top performance. This shoe even has air bags in the soles, shown with an arrow, for good cushioning.*

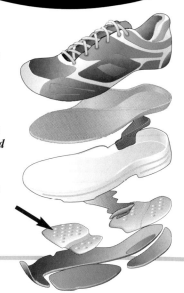

Shoes with loose heels can cause ankle problems.

▲ In the future, genetic researchers may improve racehorses by selecting genes for perfect muscles. There are dangers with this. One of these genes may also cause paralysis.

Taking drugs to win events

Using drugs to gain a winning edge in sports goes back to the 1950s. In 1954 Russian weight lifters at the Olympic Games were reported to be using anabolic steroids – drugs to build up their muscles, far beyond what would be possible by ordinary practice.

Today, there are a wide variety of performance-enhancing drugs that are banned from sports. Many build up muscles while others improve stamina, to go farther in long-distance events. Beta-blockers are drugs that slow the heartbeat. They are useful in sports when a steady hand is needed, such as for target shooting.

Testing for drugs at the Olympics started at the Mexico City Games in 1968, but muscle-building drugs were not banned until 1975. It was not until 1983 that a method for testing drug use was developed. The method is still used for checking athletes today.

In every sport, the materials and equipment have been studied and improved to help athletes do their best. For example, speed skaters use skates with special blades that stay on the ice longer for more speed. Pole vaulters use glass-fiber poles that are more flexible than older designs. For runners, special tracks help out, with a slightly springy surface that helps conserve energy. Swimmers benefit from wearing body suits. Such suits have fine grooves, like the skin of dolphins and sharks. The grooves allow water to slide past smoothly, so a swimmer can reach higher speeds.

▲ A man from Finland has a gene that gives him a high number of oxygen-bearing red blood cells, allowing him to excel at cross-country skiing.

▶ Researchers do not know the exact genetic makeup of what makes a good runner – special muscle types and extra-efficient lungs are just two of many factors.

Biomechanics is the name for the scientific ways of improving performance. The best athletes can improve their performance because they have learned to focus or concentrate well. Research shows that thinking about other things before the event helps take away nervousness – which might be just what is needed to beat a good competitor. Being able to relax is important. Stress tightens up muscles, making them less efficient.

A good training program allows an athlete to concentrate for a rocket-like start

What's next?

Biotech is a rapidly changing area of science, where breakthroughs are being made almost every day. What can we expect in the future?

▲ *Genetic testing helps endangered species, such as the southern humpback whale.*

Many animal species are in danger, some because they are hunted for their meat or skins, others because humans take over the areas where they live. One way science can help endangered species is by checking their genetic patterns.

The humpback whale is still hunted by some whalers, even though it is illegal. When the meat is sold in stores, it looks like other meat. To help save these whales, biotech researchers take small samples of the meat, to make a complete DNA pattern. This way, meat can be checked in stores and whalers who sell the illegal meat can be caught and prosecuted.

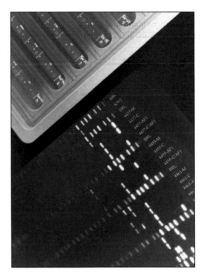

◀ *Getting samples is only one part of whale tracking. Samples, photographs, and many other details have to be matched up to provide a complete set of data.*

Biotech companies are based mostly in North America and Europe, but other countries could provide valuable information. For example, India has a treasure chest of resources which could be used for medical and ecological breakthroughs. One state alone has 5000 species of flowering plants. Traditional healers use these local plants to treat patients.

▲ *A good way for people to stay in shape will still be to eat foods with plenty of natural ingredients.*

◀ *This single-cell creature is shown magnified millions of times. Some of these produce useful substances. One of these may lower the risk of heart disease.*

The biotech body

Transplanting healthy body organs to a patient was first tried in the 1960s. Since then, researchers have come up with many ways to repair or replace failed and damaged body parts. On this computer-generated image is a roundup of some replacements used today, and ideas for the near future.

Partial deafness is treated today by traditional hearing aids or implants. A tiny computer sound sensor could be placed in the ear to help people who are completely deaf.

Poor eyesight is often treated by laser surgery and blindness by implants. Future treatments include light-sensing electronic implants at the back of the eye, with a direct nerve link to the brain.

The most advanced prosthetic limbs today are wired to the nervous system. Future prosthetics may use tiny computers to link the limb directly to the brain. This would make control almost as quick and natural as as in natural limbs.

Bones can be encouraged to mend by injecting growth material into the area where the bone was broken. In the future, bones may regrow through special scaffold material, which bridges the broken areas. When the bone has finished growing the scaffold dissolves away.

Will there be head transplants?

Researchers have already transplanted a monkey's head onto another body. It survived for several days, although it was paralyzed from the neck down as scientists cannot yet repair nerve tissue like the spinal cord.

Other experiments have used signals from a monkey's brain to move a robot. With robotic limbs, this may be a better solution for people who are paralyzed.

An organ that has failed can sometimes be replaced by a machine. In 2000, British heart patient Peter Houghton was fitted with a turbine heart pump. In the future, hearts, livers, and kidneys may be grown in a laboratory, using cells taken from the patient's body. When ready, the new organ would be transplanted into the patient.

Small sections of skin can heal easily, but losing a large area of skin in a fire is much more serious, and may need a transplant of skin from another part of the patient's body. In the future, skin will be grown in the laboratory from starter cells taken from the patient, and transplanted when ready.

Veins and arteries can be grown in the laboratory from starter cells taken from pigs. In the future, these blood vessels are likely to be started from cells taken from the patient's own body.

27

Time track

A list of some important dates in biotech research, from the work of early pioneers to the human genome and into the future.

▲ A Roman archer with a wooden leg is featured in a mosaic in France.

Ancient Greece   In 1500 B.C., the physician Hippocrates finds that willow bark can dull headaches and other pains.

Ancient Rome   Romans make prosthetic limbs for soldiers who have lost arms and legs in battle.

1608   Zacharias Jansen from Holland invents the microscope.

1665   English scientist Robert Hooke studies objects with a microscope and finds that living things are made from cells.

1822   Gregor Mendel is born. After years of study, he formulates the laws of inheritance, which predict how living things will grow. His ideas are published in 1865.

1831   Charles Darwin from England sets out on HMS *Beagle* to survey the coast of South America. During mainland visits, Darwin finds *fossils*, which show that some species die out while others survive.

1831   Scottish botanist Robert Brown finds that cells have a tiny speck inside. He calls it the nucleus.

▲ Medicines and microscope from the early 1900s.

◀ From figs to frogs, all life on Earth uses DNA as its code.

1838   German botanist Matthias Schlieden shows that plants as well as animals are made from cells. In the same year, Karl von Nageli from Switzerland sees tiny strands in the cell. They are later called "chromosomes."

1842   A general anesthetic is used for the first time in an operation to keep the patient unconscious while surgery is being carried out.

1859   Charles Darwin publishes *On the Origin of Species*. He claims that living species may change over time to fit with changes in their environment. He also suggests the idea of evolution from simpler forms of life millions of years ago.

1899   The German company Bayer starts producing aspirin as a painkilling drug.

1907   American scientist Thomas Hunt Morgan produces the first chromosome map, showing genes in fruit flies.

1932   *Electron microscope* uses beams of electron particles instead of light rays, to allow great magnifications.

1953   James Watson from the U.S. and Francis Crick from England show that DNA is shaped like a "double helix," or double spiral. DNA is the carrier of the genetic code used by all living things on Earth.

1954   Soviet weightlifters use special drugs to boost their performance at the Olympic Games.

1960s   Organ transplants are carried out by Dr. Christiaan Barnard in South Africa. They show problems created by the body's natural defenses, notably *rejection* of foreign tissues.

1960s   Many crops are specially bred for better growth. It is called the "green revolution." New chemicals control pests well, but many insects develop resistance to these chemicals after a few years.

► *This machine is used to extract DNA from white blood cells.*

1973 U.S. researchers Herbert Boyer and Stanley Cohen experiment with recombinant DNA. They take sections of DNA from different bacteria, joining them together again in a new pattern.

1980 First patent granted on a living thing, a micro-organism made to digest waste from oil spills at sea.

1981 A gene is moved from one animal species to another.

1988 Special type of mouse patented for use in research projects

1990 Genes are used to treat a girl with a weak immune defense system. Injections with undamaged DNA boost her body's ability to resist disease.

1990 Human Genome Organization (HUGO) started in October. Thousands of scientists from across the world try to map out all the genes in human DNA.

1992 Genetically modified (GM) crops are planted in China.

1994 First GM food on sale. The Flavr Savr tomato has changes that allow it to ripen on the vine without softening.

1994 First gene theft, when two men try to steal cells from a laboratory. The cells have a gene that could help failing human kidneys.

1996 A team of researchers in Scotland clone a sheep called Dolly. This is the first mammal to be cloned.

1996 Genome of brewer's yeast published. It is the most complex organism so far decoded by HUGO.

1998 Scientists in Hawaii create mouse clones. They also create clones of these clones. The factory-like lab can produce as many as 200 clones in a day.

2000 First draft of the human genome is published.

2000 Peter Houghton becomes the first human to be fitted with a battery-powered turbine heart.

2001 Heritage GeneBank formed, to preserve the genes of endangered and rare species.

Into the future
2005 Human genome completely mapped and sequenced.

2010 Widespread testing to check for the risk of cancer, diabetes and strokes, as well as genetic checks on pregnant mothers to make sure their babies will be healthy. Wide use of laboratory pigs as organ donors, following their earlier use to supply heart valves.

2015 Medicine specially made for each person's particular genetic makeup.

2015 Tissue banks become common, with organs grown to order in the laboratory.

2030 Most people in the U.S. live healthily for 85 years or more. This compares to a usual lifespan of just 47 years in 1900, and 76 years in 1999.

2040 An active human lifespan of 120-150 years becomes possible as researchers find out many secrets of cell repair and old age diseases.

2050 GM humans with cloned body parts become common.

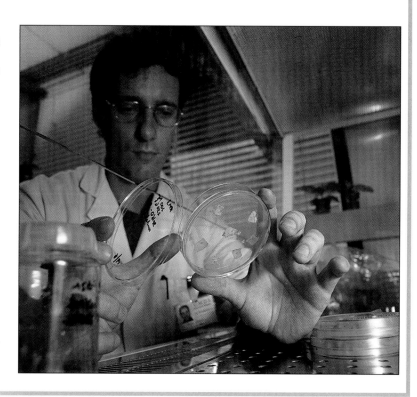

► *A researcher checks on the progress of GM plants in the laboratory.*

Glossary

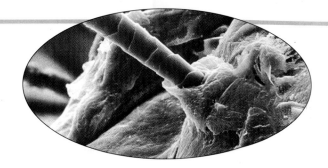

A n explanation of the technical terms and concepts in this book.

AIDS
A virus referred to by letters that stand for Acquired Immune Deficiency Syndrome. The body of an AIDS sufferer cannot fight off micro-organisms. It is caused by HIV (Human Immunodeficiency Virus).

Alzheimer's disease
Brain disease that causes loss of memory and other mental problems, especially in older people.

▲ *Corn is the world's most widely grown GM crop.*

Anabolic steroid
Type of drug used to build up body tissue, for extra bulk and muscle. First used by weightlifters in the 1954 Olympic Games, but now illegal.

Anesthetic
A gas or drug that is given to a patient so that they lose sensations of pain or touch. A general anesthetic makes a patient unconscious.

Antiseptic
A liquid or spray that kills bacteria. First used by Sir Joseph Lister during surgery in the 1800s.

Artery
Any one of the tubes that carry blood from the heart. Veins are the tubes that carry blood back to the heart.

Bacteria
Single-cell organisms that reproduce by dividing. Many types cause diseases, but other bacteria, such as those that change milk to yogurt, are useful.

Cancer
A group of cells that grows and spreads rapidly out of control.

Cell
The basic living unit. Some organisms are single cells, but most plants and animals are made of many cells of different shapes and sizes. Typically, a cell consists of a watery, jelly-like substance called cytoplasm, surrounded by a membrane that gives the cell its shape. In the middle is a nucleus.

▼ *DNA sample in a test tube.*

▲ *Ultra-close work is done mainly with the electron microscope.*

Chromosome
Microscopic threads inside the nucleus of a cell that carry DNA and genes. Humans have 22 pairs of chromosomes plus a pair that determine sex. We all have the same number of chromosomes, but our slightly different genes make us individuals.

Clone
In the laboratory, a living creature made without sexual reproduction that is genetically identical to only one parent. Various clones can be made by biotechnologists – from frogs and mice to sheep and goats.

DNA
Short for DeoxyriboNucleic Acid, the molecule that makes up chromosomes and genes. It is shaped as two long spiral threads, coiled around each other.

Electron microscope
Type of microscope with strong magnifying power. It uses a beam of electrons, instead of light rays.

Embryo
Name for the early stages of a fertilized egg, as it divides and grows. When it grows larger it is usually called a fetus.

Fossil
A stone impression of a living thing that died thousands of years ago. Fossils of many life forms have been found, from ancient fish to large dinosaurs.

Gene
Coded message stored along the DNA of a chromosome. Gene sequences provide the pattern for life – from the size of your foot, to the color of your hair.

Genetic engineering
Changing the genes of a living organism in a laboratory. Genes are moved from one set to another.

Genome
All the genes in a cell. Each type of living thing has its own genome, ranging from simple ones in flies to more complex ones in humans and other mammals.

GM
Short for Genetically Modified, anything from disease-resistant wheat to a mouse made for laboratory tests.

Hair cell
One of thousands of tiny hair-like cells in the ears. Human hair cells cannot replace themselves if damaged.

Immune system
The body's defense against infections. Antibodies are produced by white blood cells, and attack bacteria and viruses.

Keyhole surgery
Operation through a tiny hole in the body. Robot equipment may be used, because the tools can be made very small.

Mammal
Animal that is warm-blooded, gives birth to live young, and feeds its babies with mother's milk. Examples include sheep, cows, cats, dogs, and humans.

Molecule
Group of atoms arranged in various ways. A water molecule has two hydrogen atoms and one of oxygen. DNA molecules may have from 100,000 to 10 million atoms, depending on the organism.

Nano
Literally, one thousand-millionth part of something. Used today to describe any ultra-small machine or system.

Nucleus
The life center of a cell, containing DNA. Genetic instructions carried by the DNA control the way the body works.

Nutraceutical
A food which combines nutrition with pharmaceutical properties. For example, a GM potato may have added drug genes.

Organic food
Crops or animals which have been raised in natural, healthy conditions. Examples include hens that are free to walk in the open air and crops that have not been sprayed with chemicals.

Papillae
Small bulges of flesh, occurring at hair roots or on the tongue. Taste buds are on many tongue papillae.

Pharmaceutical
Another word for medicine, from the ancient Greek word *pharmakon*.

Prosthetic
Any artificial replacement for a missing limb, such as a robotic hand or leg.

Protein
Organic compound that is found in living things. There are thousands of proteins, each with a different job. Muscles are made almost entirely of protein.

Rejection
Non-acceptance by the body of organs transplanted from another person or an animal. The body's immune system may treat the new tissue as an invader and attack it. Drugs are used to keep this defense under control.

Retina
Coating in the back of the eye. Cells called rods and cones sense light coming through the pupil, and send signals along the optic nerve to the brain. The brain translates the signals into a moving view of the world.

Sensor
Any mechanical device that can see, hear, touch, smell or taste. Some sensors are not as good as human senses, others are more sensitive.

Species
A group of living things such as dogs, cats, or humans that breed among themselves and have young.

Stem cell
Stem cells are undifferentiated – they are not a particular type of cell. They develop into different cells, such as those for skin, bone, eye, heart and other body parts.

Telomere
Telomeres are caps protecting the ends of chromosomes. They may be connected with cell aging because they shorten each time a cell divides.

Transplant
The surgical transfer of a healthy organ, such as a heart or kidney, from one body to another.

Ulcer
An open sore which damages tissue. Typical places for ulcers are on the stomach lining and in the mouth.

Virus
Tiny infective agent that usually causes disease. It invades a cell, turning it into a virus production center. The cell bursts, and new viruses spread to other cells.

X-ray
Type of radiation that can pass through solid objects such as flesh. Used in medicine to check inside the body. Other types of radiation include light, radio, TV and microwaves.

▲ *Animals in a species can breed only with each other. For example, lions belong to the cat family, but do not breed with other cat species such as the puma or cheetah.*

▼ *An X-ray photograph of a foot shows the bones clearly. Flesh shows only faintly.*

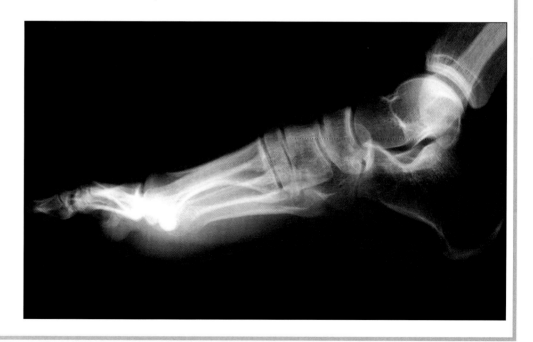

Index

A
Africa 23
aging 31
AIDS virus 23, 30
Alzheimer's disease 22, 30
ancient Greece, Greeks 8, 28
ancient Rome, Romans 10, 28
anesthetics 4, 28, 30
antiseptics 4, 30
arteries 12, 27, 30
artificial limbs 10
Asia 23
athletes 2, 24, 25

B
bacteria 4, 17, 29, 30, 31
Bayer 8, 28
biomechanics 2, 25
bionics 2
BioSteel 16
blindness 14, 27
blood 2, 10, 30
bones 5, 6, 11, 27, 31
brain 10, 11, 13, 14, 15, 22, 27,
    30, 31
breathing bag 21

C
cancer 9, 22, 29, 30
cattle, cows 21, 29
cells 2, 3, 6, 14, 22, 27, 28, 29,
    30, 31
    eye 14
    hair 15, 31
    red blood 25
    smell 14
    stem 6, 31
China 29
chromosomes 6, 19, 28, 30, 31
clean rooms 17
clones 16, 17, 19, 29, 30
computer chips 14
computer images, scans, 13
computers 9, 10, 11, 12, 13, 27

D
da Vinci robot 12-13
Darwin, Charles 28
deafness 15, 27
disease 4, 5, 7, 20, 22, 29, 30, 31
DNA 2, 6, 26, 28, 29, 30, 31
drugs, medicines 2, 4, 5, 8-9, 13,
    16, 20, 21, 22, 23, 24, 25,
    29, 30, 31
    anabolic steroids 25, 30
    aspirin 8, 28

beta-blockers 25
    Zantac 9
drug trials 9

E
ears 6, 31
electron microscope see microscope
embryos 17, 30
endangered species 26
Europe 23, 26
evolution 28
eyes 6, 14, 31
eyesight 27

F
fossils 28, 30
FreeHand 11
fruit flies 7, 18, 28

G
Galapagos giant tortoise 18
genes 2, 7, 15, 17, 19, 20, 22, 25,
    28, 29, 30
genetic engineering 2, 30
genome 7, 31
    human 28, 29
GM products 7, 20, 21, 29, 31

H
hearing 15
hearing aids 15, 27
heart 2, 10, 20, 26, 27, 29, 30, 31
Heritage GeneBank 29
hip replacements 11
Hippocrates 8, 28
HIV 23, 30
Hooke, Robert 6, 28
Human Genome Organization
    (HUGO) 17, 29

I
immune system 31
implants 14, 27
India 26

J
Jansen, Zacharias 6, 28
Japan 14

K
kidneys 27, 29, 31

L
Lister, Sir Joseph 4, 30
liver 27
long life 18-19

M
medicines see drugs
medicines, alternative 23
Mendel, Gregor 28
mice 19, 29
microscope 6, 28, 30
monkeys 11, 27
muscles 11, 20, 25

N
nanomachines 13
nano-sub 12, 13
nerve 11, 27
New Zealand 29
North America 20, 23, 26, see also
    United States
nutraceuticals 20, 21, 31

O
olfactory receptor ("smell cell") 14
Olympic Games 25, 28, 30
oxygen 19, 25

P
papillae 15, 31
pharmaceutical 31
pharmaceutical companies 8-9
pigs 27, 29
prosthetics 2, 10, 11, 27, 28, 31

R
refrigeration 21
rejection 31
retina 14, 31
robots 9, 12-13, 17, 27, 31
Roentgen, Wilhelm 5

S
senses 14-15, 31
sharks 15, 25
sheep 16, 29
sight 14
skin 5, 27, 31
skull 13
South Africa 28
spider silk 16
spinal cord 27
spine 11
sports 24-25
    equipment 2, 24, 25
    materials 24, 25
stress 18, 25
surgeon, surgery 4, 5, 12, 13, 28,
    30, 31
    laser 27
    keyhole 12, 31

T
taste 15
taste buds 31
teeth 5, 12
telomeres 19, 31
tongue 15
transplants 27, 28, 31

U
ulcers 31
    stomach 9
United States 22, 29, see also North
    America

V
veins 27, 30
virus 23, 31

X
X-ray 5, 31

Acknowledgements
We wish to thank all those individuals and
organizations that have helped create this
publication.

Photographs were supplied by:
Alpha Archive
F. Bayer and Co
Robert Becker
Juergen Berger
Dr. Tony Brain
Custom Medical Stock Photo
Eye of Science
Malcolm Fielding
J. Greenberg
James King-Holmes
Johnson Matthey Plc
Kairos, Latin Stock
Max-Planke Institute
Peter Menzel
NMPFT
David Parker
J.C. Revy
Ron Sanford
Science & Society Picture Library
Science Museum London
Science Photo Library
Geoff Tompkinson
Volker Steger
Wellcome Trust Photo Library

Digital art created by:
Gavin Page